CARTIER
Finder of the St. Lawrence

CARTIER

FINDER OF THE ST. LAWRENCE

By RONALD SYME

Illustrated by WILLIAM STOBBS

WILLIAM MORROW AND COMPANY
New York   1958

Away to the westward, high mountains towered up from the sea. They looked cold and ugly against the gray Atlantic sky. Their crests and sides were covered with deep white snow.

Young Jacques Cartier gazed curiously at this distant land from the wet and heaving deck of his father's fishing boat. He knew he was looking at the east coast of Newfoundland. This was the year 1507, and Christopher Columbus had discovered America fifteen years ago, just about the time Jacques was born. Men no longer were afraid to sail across the Western Ocean, and now the sturdy European fishermen came to the shallow seas off Newfoundland in search of cod.

One thing always annoyed Jacques and disappointed him. His companions aboard the ship were not interested in taking a closer look at the nearby coast of Newfoundland or the unexplored coastline to the north and south. They used the mountains only as a guide to lead them to the best fishing grounds.

"We're here to fill our nets with good cod to feed the people of France," Jacques' father said to him. "What would we gain by sailing up and down the dangerous coast yonder? Answer that question, my son."

"We would be able to see a new country," Jacques replied. "A country where no European has ever been. We could be the first."

His father smiled and glanced at the great trawl net towed from the stern of the heavy wooden boat. "Such knowledge would not pay our crew's wages. I know that the Spaniards were lucky enough to find great wealth in the West Indian islands, but there is nothing like that among those barren mountains over there. No doubt there are wild savages, but what have they of value to exchange with good Christian men like us? Would you risk our boat, Jacques? Close to shore there are dangerous channels, where the cold sea fog hides shoals and rocks from the eyes of seamen. Our wealth lies in the good salt water beneath our keel. With nets and deep-sea lines we can find enough profit for ourselves. We have no need to go exploring."

Jacques Cartier always forgot Newfoundland when the fishing fleet hastened back to France at the end of the summer. He was glad to return to the stone quays and narrow

streets of the little fishing port of St. Malo. It was a pleasant change for him to sleep in a comfortable bed ashore and to sit in front of a blazing fire on chilly nights. Yet when spring came, and the fishing boats set out across the Atlantic again, Jacques remembered those mountains. They were like old friends he looked forward to seeing after a long absence.

The years went by. Jacques Cartier still sailed westward to the Newfoundland Banks every spring and back to France in the autumn. Not once did he manage to reach those snow-covered mountains. He was thirty years old when he heard that at last someone had explored the eastern coast of North America.

The man was John Verrazano, a plucky Italian sea captain. Verrazano groped his way northward along the North American coast until he reached the southern end of New-foundland. During his travels he met friendly

Indian tribes and thought he saw traces of gold on the shores of a vast bay which later became New York Harbor. After his return to Europe, Verrazano said that the coast, from what is now Virginia to Maine, was "full of pine trees, bay trees, and high cypress trees, and many other sorts of trees unknown in Europe. It is a most rich and fertile land. One can smell its sweet fragrance even when far out to sea."

When he heard of this voyage Cartier suddenly remembered his boyhood dreams. He longed to see the land of splendid forests and unknown tribes of Indians. But now he was captain of his own fishing boat. He knew that the crew would not give up their wages while they went exploring Newfoundland, and he did not have enough money saved to pay them.

Cartier became weary of the North Atlantic's wild weather and the hard toil of fishing.

He decided to become captain of a big trading vessel which was bound for the jungle-
covered shores of Brazil, in South America.
He had heard that the Indians down there
would exchange a handful of pearls for a steel-
bladed knife. And that sometimes they offered
the clumsy gold ornaments they wore to get a
small mirror or a couple of fishhooks.

Fish will never bring me enough profit to
pay for a voyage of discovery, Cartier thought

to himself. I must find wealth some other way. Perhaps I can do it in this country of Brazil.

But he was unlucky in South America. Too many other ships had been there already. The natives were learning the real value of their pearls, and they had sold all their gold ornaments to other seamen. Cartier made little profit and returned to France feeling very disappointed. He paid no attention when his crew told friends ashore that he was the best seaman afloat.

"Captain Cartier can grope his way through any fog and come safely to land," the seamen declared. "Aye, and he made sure we were well fed and got good pay on his ship. Whenever Captain Cartier wants another crew, we'll be glad to sail with him."

The sailors' words reached the ears of a great and powerful man in France. His name was Brion-Chabot. Although he was no seaman, Brion-Chabot was in charge of the

whole French navy. He was friendly with the king and they spent much time together playing tennis or hunting deer.

Count Brion-Chabot was very interested in ships and exploration. He knew all about the voyage Verrazano had made. Often he wondered if a sea passage of some kind led across America from east to west. Such a channel, he thought, would mean that ships from Europe could reach the Pacific Ocean and the rich spice islands of the East Indies very quickly. At present vessels had to sail thousands of miles around Africa and across the Indian Ocean to get there. In those days many seamen thought that there might be a waterway across America. It was quite possible, they said, that Verrazano had just missed the entrance to it.

Brion-Chabot decided to meet this popular Captain Cartier and called him to the king's palace. The count gazed curiously at the stocky, bearded, broad-shouldered man who was said to be the best sea captain in all France.

Cartier did not waste words when he spoke. His seafaring life had not given him the gracious manners usually expected in a royal palace. His dark eyes looked at Brion-Chabot in a very honest manner, and he did not seem in the least nervous at finding himself in the king's own palace. "Yes, my lord," said Car-

tier. "I have heard stories about a sea road from the Atlantic to the Pacific."

"Do you believe the stories are true?" Brion-Chabot asked him.

Cartier shrugged his big shoulders. "The channel is worth looking for," he replied. "But—begging your pardon, my lord—the only things I know to be true are those I have seen with my own eyes."

Brion-Chabot frowned a little. "You do not seem very enthusiastic, Captain," he said. "I hoped to hear more cheerful words from you."

Cartier looked squarely at the richly dressed nobleman. "My lord," he said, "if a man watches the sky while he is walking, he will not see the ground beneath his feet. You look for some waterway across America. I remember what Captain Verrazano told us about that country before he was hanged by the Spaniards for sailing into their Caribbean Sea. He said it was a land rich in furs and forests, and perhaps gold as well. Surely these things are as important as a waterway! France might be wise to take North America as her own colony, even if there is *no* sea passage from east to west."

No one had spoken to Brion-Chabot like this before. It might mean a year or two in prison for being rude to one of the most powerful men in the country. But the High Admiral of France could recognize a brave and honest man when he saw one. He thought that sturdy little Captain Cartier spoke with good sense.

Brion-Chabot leaned back in his gilded chair. The angry expression disappeared from his face. "Then go and find out more about this country of North America," he ordered. "First search for a waterway from ocean to ocean; then bring back a full report of everything you see for yourself. Your work will be rewarded by King Francis."

Cartier remained where he was. "My lord,"

he said, "cod fishing does not bring wealth to men like myself. I would be glad to obey your commands, but I cannot afford to pay for a voyage of discovery."

Brion-Chabot made an impatient gesture with his hands. "Do not worry about money," he said. "This time, Captain, France will pay for your ships and sailors."

Forty-two-year-old Jacques Cartier sailed from St. Malo in April, 1534. His two little schooners weighed only sixty tons each, but their masts carried triangular sails, like those of a modern sailboat. This made the ships quick and easy to handle in dangerous waters. About thirty hardy French fishermen formed the crew of each ship.

Cartier soon saw the mountains of Newfoundland rising above the horizon. This time, however, he kept his vessels sailing toward the distant mountains. "We will anchor off the

coast," he told the seamen. "With luck, we will find plenty to eat ashore."

Cartier was right. An enormous number of sea birds came yearly to build their nests on the tiny islets off the coast of Newfoundland. The men rowed their boats through winter ice which had not yet melted. Among the rocks they caught and ate guillemots, puffins, and great auks. The called the auks *pingouin,* meaning fat. Three hundred years later there

21

were no great auks left alive in the world, and other men gave the name *penguin* to the bird which lives near the South Pole.

Sometimes when the sailors were catching birds, they came face to face with polar bears, which had swum out to the islets. The first time this happened, the men fled wildly. They described the bears as "fierce beasts, as large as cows and as white as swans." Soon they learned to shoot these animals with their clumsy guns, and then they ate fried bear steaks instead of oily-tasting sea birds. Near the northern end of Newfoundland Cartier sighted other animals, which he said were "like oxen, but have two tusks in the mouth, similar to those of the elephant." These were walruses, which were often seen around Newfoundland in those days.

Cartier reached the northern tip of Newfoundland and saw a foggy channel stretching westward.

Perhaps my lord Brion-Chabot is right, he said to himself. This may be the mouth of the great channel which leads to the Pacific Ocean. He steered into the opening, which afterward became known as the Strait of Belle Isle.

A small birch-bark canoe appeared suddenly in the mist ahead of the carefully moving ships. Two young Indians stared up in terror at the great monsters of wood and canvas gliding toward them.

The French seamen gazed down curiously at these brown-skinned savages, whose heads were shaved, except for a top lock, and who wore nothing but waistcloths of marten fur.

"Do not frighten them," said Cartier. "Smile, so they will see we are friends."

The Indians may have felt a little less frightened when they saw bearded faces grinning down at them over the sides of the ships. More likely they were tempted by the

meat and biscuits which Cartier held out to them. They obeyed his signs to climb aboard the vessel and made no fuss when their canoe was lifted onto the deck.

"They made me understand," wrote Cartier, "that they had come to this part of the sea on a fishing trip from somewhere to the west."

The two vessels began to grope their way

down the channel along the west coast of Newfoundland. The Indians soon became used to their new quarters. They ate enormously and amused themselves by trying on the crew's jerseys, woollen caps, and homespun shirts.

Cartier reached the northern end of Prince Edward Island at the beginning of August. His ships dropped anchor in a sheltered little bay. The crew, weary after so much time afloat and eager for a change of food, gazed eagerly at forests of juniper and pine, beech and maple. They rowed ashore and wandered through grassy meadows, munching handfuls of red currants, gooseberries, ripe ears of Indian corn, and delicious strawberries.

The sailors were ready to spend the rest of the summer on this peaceful island. But Cartier was not the kind of man to waste time on his own comfort. He enjoyed the warm sunshine and the pigeons his men shot in the

The Voyages
of
Jacques Cartier

St Lawrence R.

Chaleur Bay

R. of Cap Rouge

STADACONA (QUEBEC)

Charles R.

1541

1535

Isle of Orleans

Hochelaga (Montreal)

Lachine Rapids

0   100   200 Miles

Strait of Belle Isle

to France

from France

nsti I.

Gulf of St. Lawrence

Newfoundland

Cabot Strait

Atlantic Ocean

nce
ward
I.

a

→ - → - → - → - → First Voyage 1534
• • • • • • • • • • • • • • • Second Voyage 1535

forests and roasted, but he knew that he had only reached the frontier of an immense country and that the summer was drawing swiftly to an end.

He sailed on westward, hoping he followed a channel which led into the heart of the land. But, by mistake, he entered Chaleur Bay, where he sailed around and around, trying to find the sea passage to the west.

A party of Indians saw the white sails of his ships on the distant sea. They came streaking out in canoes to meet the vessels, yelling and whooping. The Indians seemed so friendly that Cartier decided to risk going ashore to their village.

"They have no weapons in sight," he said to the men with him. "However, we must be careful not to anger them in any way. Let every man hide a knife or pistol under his jersey. Then we, too, will appear to be unarmed."

On shore the amazed, curious Indians touched the white skins and pulled gently at the beards of the Frenchmen. They yelled orders to the women and girls who were peeping at the visitors from a distance. Cartier and his men soon found themselves seated on bark mats laid on the ground. They were handed wooden bowls containing *migane,* a kind of porridge made from crushed Indian corn mixed with dried fish.

"It smelt very queerly," Cartier noted, "for some of the fish was bad. My men made strange faces as they ate. And the other food these poor savages gave us tasted even worse. Yet because we wished to please them, we ate everything and smiled all the time."

The Indians were less pleased with their guests when Cartier's men started putting up a tall wooden cross on the shore. It was intended as a sign to other explorers that Frenchmen had already visited Chaleur Bay. Fastened to the cross was a leaden plate bearing the words: *God Save the King of France.*

The Indians guessed rightly that Cartier was claiming their country for himself. They clustered around the Frenchmen, shaking their heads. A few of them went to their tents and came back with bows and stone-headed tomahawks.

But Cartier was a clever fellow at making himself understood by sign language. "I ex-

plained to them," he wrote, "that this cross was only a mark, so that I might find Chaleur Bay next time I visited the coast."

The Indians believed this story. They crowded to the shore and offered presents of food and furs when the Frenchmen were ready to return to their ships. But they uttered howls of grief when the two Indian fishermen who had first met the French prepared to go away with the white strangers.

Heavy white fog was rolling across the sea when Cartier sailed out of Chaleur Bay. He saw that he must not delay any longer in these waters, for winter would come soon. The days were growing shorter and the nights were cold. He turned northward and steered for Belle Isle passage, and the Atlantic.

The ships were off the coast of Anticosti Island when a morning of hot sunshine dissolved the clammy fog. Cartier was delighted to see a fine wide channel stretching westward. Unbroken forests of dark-green pine reached down to the shore. He gazed at this splendid waterway for a while, and then he turned his back on it.

"Yonder lies a sea road we have found too late," he said. "Next year we will come back to discover where it leads."

Two very surprised young Indians found themselves sailing away from their native land. They had no idea where they were going and began to weep. They did not recover their good spirits until Cartier's ships were plunging across the Atlantic toward the distant coast of France.

As soon as Cartier had docked at St. Malo he went to see Brion-Chabot.

"Tell me about this passage you sighted to the west," said the young High Admiral. "Do you think it leads to the Pacific Ocean, my good Captain?"

"Sir," Cartier replied, "no man knows how a road may end until he has traveled along it. You have asked me a question I cannot answer."

Brion-Chabot sighed. "You are always just the same, Captain! Yet I find your honesty pleasant after all the false, smooth talk one hears in this palace. You seem to bring the healthy winds of your cold ocean with you. Now I have fresh orders for you. The king has already heard of the discoveries you have made. He commands you to sail again in the spring of next year. Bring us back an answer to the mystery of that channel you saw when the fog rolled aside."

"By your leave, sir," said Cartier, "I would ask for more men and larger ships. If the voyage goes well, I will spend next winter in that country across the sea. Sixty men and a few barrels of salted beef, such as I had this year, are not enough."

Brion-Chabot tried to hide a smile. The fishermen of St. Malo loved to drive a hard bargain, and Captain Cartier was no different from the rest of them. "How many ships?" he asked. "And how many men?"

"Three vessels and a hundred sailors in the crew," Cartier answered.

Brion-Chabot nodded. "Less than I thought you would ask for, Captain. I will see you get them."

Cartier left St. Malo again in the spring of 1535. His largest vessel was 140 tons, which was a fairly large ship in those days. The smallest was a little fishing trawler of only forty tons. Aboard these three ships were 112 sturdy fishermen who had made many voyages already to the fishing grounds of Newfoundland.

The two young Indians also sailed with Cartier. They were delighted with their stay in France, where they had eaten good food

and slept in beds warmer than any their
countrymen had ever known. After nine
months in St. Malo they had learned to speak
and understand the French language fairly
well. Now they would be valuable to Cartier
as interpreters. Their only worry was whether
their tribe would believe the stories they had
to tell of the wonderful things they had seen
in France.

Bad weather delayed Cartier's ships. It

took five weeks to sail from St. Malo to Newfoundland. Huge waves smashed against the
vessels, causing them to roll and plunge with
dangerous violence. The force of the wind
ripped canvas sails from the masts and burst
the stout ropes of the rigging. Boats on the
deck were washed away, and men had to
work the big hand-operated pumps to keep
down the water which was always leaking
into the holds.

Somehow or other, Cartier managed to find his way across the Atlantic. His three battered, leaking ships crept past the northern coast of Newfoundland and entered Belle Isle Strait.

When the vessels reached the rocky black shores of Anticosti Island and the beginning of the waterway to the west, the Indians ran to the bow of Cartier's ship. They started talking excitedly as they pointed toward the distant shore. "This is our country," they said. "Nearby lies the province we call *Saguenay* in our own language. Ahead of us is another province, named *Canada*. Many canoe journeys beyond that is a third province called *Hochelaga*. If you sail up this river, you will come to the village of Stadacona. Our chieftain, Donnacona, lives there with his tribe."

"Are you sure this is a river?" Cartier asked them. "Are its waters salt or fresh?"

"Fresh," the Indians replied. "You will

leave the bitter water of the ocean far behind you."

Cartier knew from this that he had not found a way to the Pacific Ocean. This channel was merely some enormous river which, sooner or later, would come to an end. For a while he stayed silent, and his weather-darkened face was grim. Yet presently his courage and good spirits returned. He gazed at the unending forests and fine stretches of natural meadow and saw that this was a fertile country. Here was land enough for all the poor, hard-working peasants of France.

Cartier named the mighty stream the River of Hochelaga, and sometimes he referred to it as the Great River of Canada. In later years the name was changed to the St. Lawrence River.

Because he was a skillful navigator, Cartier managed to avoid all the shoals and treacherous eddies which threatened to wreck

his ships as they sailed up the river. Often he
perched himself on a mast, high above the
deck, so that he could watch for the perils
which lay hidden beneath the river's surface.
Whenever he saw danger ahead, he shouted
orders to the steersman below.

Five hundred miles above Anticosti Island,
Cartier brought his vessels to anchor. The
ships floated in a quiet channel between high
gray cliffs and a little island, now called the

Isle of Orleans, covered with handsome trees and grape-bearing vines.

"We call this place Kebec," the Indians told Cartier. "The word means narrow in our own tongue." (French settlers later altered this Indian name to Quebec.)

Indians in the village of Stadacona saw the ships advancing up the river. They launched their canoes and came flying out from the shore. These Huron people had decorated their bare brown bodies with stripes of blue, red, and white clay. Their long black hair was ornamented with bright feathers. Clusters of wampum, beads made from the inner part of sea shells, dangled from leather straps around their necks. Some of these beads were black or violet, others white or red.

The canoes hovered around the anchored ships. None of the warriors climbed aboard the vessels until Donnacona, their chieftain, arrived. He was a tall, elderly man with a

lean hawk-nosed face and dark, heavy-lidded eyes. Without showing any sign of fear, he climbed nimbly onto the deck of Cartier's own ship.

While Donnacona sat and ate the bread and wine which Cartier placed before him, the two young Indians began telling him about the voyage they had made to France. Warriors gathered closely around, exclaiming "Ho! Ho!" in amazed voices, when they heard of carriages with wheels and houses which had roofs of slate.

Presently Donnacona pushed away his empty plate. He glanced at Cartier in a friendly way. "Tomorrow there will be a *tabagie* (feast) for you and your companions," he said through the interpreters. "Let everyone come from the ships. You are among friends. You have nothing to fear."

At the feast the Frenchmen sat on bark mats and ate bear and beaver meat, dried fish, and crushed Indian corn. Through the interpreters Cartier asked Donnacona questions about the Great River of Canada. For some reason the chieftain was not eager to let the Frenchmen go any farther.

"Devils and fearsome ghosts with horns live higher up the river," he said. "Their demon god will eat your flesh and gnaw your bones if you enter their country."

Cartier tried not to laugh. He was not scared by such stories, and he guessed that Donnacona was trying to frighten him. He wrote in his diary that this demon must be "a great fool and a noddle."

When the sailors returned to their vessels, Cartier began making his plans. "We'll leave the two larger ships here," he said. "The river seems to be growing narrower, so it might be dangerous to sail them any farther up it. I want seventy brave men to go with me in the smallest ship and our longboats. The rest of you will stay here and build a strong-walled fort. August has come, and it is too late to return to St. Malo. I have an idea that winter in this country will bring greater cold than any we have known in France."

Then Cartier went on up the River of Hochelaga with his men. "This region is as fine as anyone could wish to see," he wrote in his diary. "It is very fertile and covered with splendid trees, any one of which is tall enough to make a mainmast for my largest vessel."

The French fishermen gazed with delight at ripe bunches of grapes dangling from the vines. They watched great flocks of wild ducks feeding in the marshes and listened in wonder to the endless songs of birds among the trees. "How strange is the will of God," they said. "Here is a rich and splendid country inhabited only by poor savages who know nothing of iron or cloth, reading or writing."

On October 2, 1535, Cartier saw a lofty

mountain on an island in the river. On the
shore below the mountain was the big Indian
village of Hochelaga.

This Huron town was built in a great circle
and surrounded by a high palisade of tree
trunks. Inside the stockade was a raised plat-
form on which warriors could stand to hurl
down stones on the heads of their enemies.
There was only one gateway into the village
and not more than fifty houses. Each house

was thirty or forty yards long and ten or twelve yards wide. The walls were made of slender tree trunks, planted closely side by side and covered with sheets of bark. Light wooden beams, to which sheets of bark were cleverly lashed with strips of cured deerskin, formed the roofs. Several families lived in each house. They cooked their food on fires which burned day and night along the center of the floor.

The people of Hochelaga were more timid than those of Stadacona. They lined the shore to stare at the approaching ships, but they made no attempt to launch their canoes.

"They seem friendly enough," said Cartier, gazing at the distant crowd of brown bodies, barking dogs, and yelling children. "We will go ashore to meet them. They will think all the more of us if we wear our best and brightest clothes. But we will take our swords and long steel pikes. It will do no harm to let the people of Hochelaga understand that we can fight if we have to."

More than a thousand Indians pressed closely around Cartier and his men when they stepped ashore. For the next five days the friendly people feasted and sang almost without ceasing. At night they danced beside great bonfires which blazed in the open square of the town. Weary from overeating, the Frenchmen went to sleep every night with the noise of banging drums, barking dogs, and whooping warriors in their ears.

"These people have a very strange habit," Cartier wrote in his diary. "They dry a large kind of leaf in the sun and store it in little bags, which they wear around their necks. They also have a hollow piece of stone or wood, like a pipe. One end of this pipe they fill with the powdered leaves, which they light with a hot coal from the fire. Then they

suck the other end of the pipe, filling their bodies with smoke till it comes out of their mouths and noses like a chimney. They say this strange habit keeps them warm and in good health. I tried the smoke, but when I put the pipe in my mouth, it tasted almost as hot as pepper." Thus Cartier was one of the first explorers to describe tobacco smoking, which was still unknown in Europe.

One morning the Indians of Hochelaga be-

53

gan bringing lame, blind, and crippled people to Cartier. "They believe we can even cure all kinds of illness," said Cartier. He gazed at all the unfortunate Indians lying on the ground in front of him. "How shall I deal with them? I am not a doctor."

"Say prayers for them, Captain," suggested one of the men. "It may do some good even to heathen people, and at least it can do no harm."

Cartier stood up and stretched out one hand. He began to pray aloud in a deep, solemn voice. The vast crowd of savages stood silent with wonder, while the sick people watched with patient eyes.

"Let us climb yonder mountain," Cartier said next morning. "I have given it the name of Mont Réal (Mount Royal, from which the future city of Montreal took its name). From its summit we will be able to see across many miles of country."

High above the Indian town, Cartier and his friends looked down on an unending mantle of dark-green forest. Presently they came to a place where they could see the wide blue ribbon of the great river. Some distance above Hochelaga, the water flowed at terrible speed down rapids. The mighty flood came leaping and roaring over a three-mile flight of rocky steps. The current boiled and foamed in monstrous eddies which would de-

stroy any boat. Cartier and his friends were the first Europeans to see the Lachine Rapids above the future city of Montreal.

"There is no way of ascending those rapids in a boat," Cartier murmured to himself. "We would have to pass overland until we reached calm water above them."

A Frenchman who heard him stirred uneasily. "Captain," he said, "surely you are not thinking of going any farther up this river so late in the year? Feel how coldly the wind blows! Winter will soon come to this land, and already we are far from our comrades in the place named Kebec."

Cartier turned to the path which led back to Hochelaga. "No," he said. "I have noticed the leaves turning to red and gold and the birds flying southward. I am only wondering how our countrymen will make their overland portage past yonder rapids when they come to settle in this land."

Seventy Frenchmen climbed back into their boats and rowed away from the shore. The kindly Indians of Hochelaga lined the bank to watch their visitors depart. They uttered cries of grief as the boats began to glide downstream. A number of the younger warriors ran along the shore to keep the Frenchmen in sight as long as possible.

The men left behind at Kebec had worked fast and cleverly. A wooden fort now stood on a grassy meadow near the spot where a small river flowed into the St. Lawrence. The men used heavy timber to build a number of huts inside the wooden palisade which surrounded the fort. They carried iron stoves from the ships into these houses and split logs into great piles of firewood. October was nearly ended, and cold winds from the north warned the toiling Frenchmen to hasten their work.

Cartier inspected the fort and nodded with

satisfaction. "We will tow the ships into the mouth of this river," he said, pointing to the small river which emptied into the St. Lawrence. "If they are moored in front of our fort, we will be able to keep watch on them during the winter."

November brought the first cold weather. A blizzard came shrilling across the countryside in December. Snowdrifts rose against the walls of the fort and lay thickly on the decks of the vessels, which were now held fast by thick ice. The Frenchmen drew closer around their red-hot stoves. They marveled that any weather could be cold enough to freeze a pot of water inside a house.

"Yet so hardy were the Indians," wrote Cartier, "that they visited us almost daily in the fort. They were half-naked as usual, but it did not worry them to walk waist-deep through the frozen snow."

The Frenchmen had no supplies of fresh

food. They lived on salt meat and dried Indian corn. At the end of December illness began to spread among them. It was a disease called scurvy, brought on by lack of vegetables and fruit. Men's bodies became covered with sores, their arms and legs swelled enormously, and their teeth loosened and fell out.

Ten of Cartier's fishermen were dead when January of the year 1536 arrived. Fifteen others died that same month. The Indians stopped coming to the fort, and the two young interpreters returned to their own people. Before they left, they hinted to Cartier that the warriors in Stadacona were talking of raiding the Frenchmen's camp. "You have many things our people envy," they told Cartier. "Knives and blankets, axes, nails, and fishing lines. Guard them carefully or you may lose everything."

Cartier and three other men were still in good health. The four of them did their best

to keep a constant watch while their eighty-
three companions lay in bed, too weak from
scurvy to stand up.

One day Cartier saw a party of fifty Indians coming toward the fort. "Hammer
loudly with sticks on the floor and walls," he
said to the sick men. "Try to sing, shout, and
laugh. We must pretend we are doing some
useful work and are in good spirits."

The trick seemed to work. The Indians

heard the noise inside the fort. They paused to listen for a while and then went away. Cartier walked out of the gate after them. By this time he had learned enough of the Huron language to carry on a simple conversation.

"Wait," he called. "I have a question to ask you. One of my friends is sick. Perhaps his illness comes from the cold weather. What medicine do you use to cure such people?"

The Indians gazed at him in surprise. "We

thought that you and many of your men were ill," they said. "We were wrong, for your face is cheerful and you are well fed."

Carelessly they pointed to a spruce tree growing nearby. "There is our medicine," they said. "We strip off the bark and foliage, boil them for several hours, and drink the water while it is still warm." The Indians walked silently away, across the snowy countryside.

Cartier hurriedly fetched an ax, lopped off a number of branches from a spruce tree, and dragged them back to the fort. He and the three other men started boiling needles and bark as fast as they could.

"It was a strange but good medicine," Cartier noted. "It worked like a miracle. The men were all strong and healthy again in six days' time. By then they had drunk the whole tree!"

Spring came slowly. Each day the sun rose

a little higher above the white horizon. Piles of melting snow began rustling down from the branches of trees. Ice on the rigging of the ships began to disappear. The Frenchmen came out of the fort and walked across the meadows beside the river which they had named the St. Charles. Eagerly they chewed water-willow buds, bloodroot, and swamp-maple leaves, all of which tasted better than the sickly brew of pine needles. Later on they removed the frozen bodies of their twenty-five dead companions from snowdrifts beside the fort and buried them close to the river.

Cartier began to remember how Donnacona, the chieftain, had spoken of some distant regions of Canada where diamonds and rubies and a yellow metal like gold were to be found in the earth.

If I speak about these riches to the king, Cartier thought to himself, there is a chance I will not be believed. They may say that I have invented the stories to make sure I get more ships and money to come back here again. But if Donnacona himself tells the king what he has already told me, he will be believed. Therefore Donnacona must go back to France with us.

Then Cartier made his one bad mistake. He was deeply sorry for it ever afterward. When Donnacona visited the fort with eleven of his middle-aged friends, they were all seized by French sailors and hurried aboard the ships. Sails were hoisted and the vessels steered into midstream.

Indians, wailing with grief and fury when they saw what had happened to their chieftain, lined the bank. They shook spears and bows at the Frenchmen and howled angry threats.

"Do not hate us for what we have done," Cartier shouted to them. "I will come back next year and bring your chieftain with me.

He and his friends will be well treated in France."

Cartier believed he was speaking the truth. He really hoped to return to Canada within twelve months. But five years were to pass before he saw the River of Hochelaga again. By that time, Donnacona and the other Indians lay buried in far-off France.

Spain and France were at war with one another when Cartier reached home. The king was too busy to worry about Canada and Indian chieftains and voyages of exploration. He quarreled with Brion-Chabot and dismissed him from the royal palace. There was no one to help Cartier, and he had to go back to deep-sea fishing. He did his best to look after the Indians, and the warriors were comfortable as long as they lived. But they ate too many rich foods, wore too many clothes, and dreamed too much of their native land across the Atlantic. One by one they died, until none was left.

Only one man was still interested in Cartier's adventures across the sea. This was Count François de Roberval, a wealthy but queer-tempered aristocrat.

"You say there are plenty of good furs in that country?" he asked Cartier. "Also gold and precious stones? Well, friend Cartier, news like this interests me. We could build a trading post somewhere on the shores of the Great River of Canada and make a good profit for ourselves. I will have a word with the king about it. I think His Majesty will make me governor-general of Canada."

Cartier glanced at Roberval's hard, greedy face. He was not fond of this nobleman, who was said to be cruel, obstinate, and not very honest. But Roberval had the power and the money to arrange for another voyage.

"Very well, my lord," said Cartier. "But I

think you would do better to remain in France while I build the settlement beside the river. I know the Indians, the climate, and all the hardships we will have to face."

"Perhaps you also know where gold and diamonds are to be found," Roberval murmured craftily. "No, my good Captain, it will be better if both of us go to Canada. I will be governor; you will be my second-in-command."

The king agreed to allow Cartier to make another voyage. The war with Spain was costing a lot of money. The arrival of gold from Canada—or from anywhere else, for that matter—would be a great help to France.

In the year 1541 Cartier stood on the quay of St. Malo and gazed proudly at the five good ships of his new fleet. Another four vessels would come later, but they were still being overhauled in the nearby shipyard.

When time went by and these ships were not ready, Count Roberval became impatient at the delay and changed his mind. "Take these five ships and go," he told Cartier. "I will follow you when the other four vessels are ready for the sea."

Cartier reached Canada at the end of June. This time he entered the Gulf of St. Lawrence by Cabot Strait, at the southern end of Newfoundland. He had found this wider and safer channel when returning to France at the end of his second voyage. Vessels of all kinds have used it ever since.

A few weeks later Cartier saw once again the familiar gray cliffs rising above the dark forest. The Indian village of Stadacona had changed little since he last saw it. Canoes came out from the shore to meet the vessels when the Hurons sighted them.

"Where is our chieftain?" the warriors demanded. "Why have you taken so long to come back here? What have you done with Donnacona and our other friends?"

Cartier gazed down at the sullen faces of the warriors. He saw tomahawks and cedarwood bows in the bottoms of the canoes. He remembered that five years ago these Indians had come to meet him unarmed. Now he was having to pay for the mistake he had made in kidnapping poor Donnacona.

"Your chieftain is dead," he answered. "The others . . . well, they have married French

wives and do not want to come back here for a while."

This was a lie, of course, but Cartier feared that if he told the truth, the Indians would not believe him. They would find it hard to understand how eating too much and wearing heavy clothing had weakened their fellow countrymen's strong bodies and caused their death.

These Hurons were not fools. There was an unfriendly silence as they stared at Cartier suspiciously. Then they paddled back to the shore. This time there was no invitation for Cartier and his sea-weary company to attend a day of feasting in the village.

"They will never trust us again," Cartier muttered. "Yet when I told them that Donnacona would return in a year's time, I thought I spoke the truth. How could I know a war was coming? Could I have guessed that our king would forget me for so long? Up anchor! Hoist the sails!" he shouted. "We cannot stay here with Indians who hate us!"

The five ships went another twelve miles upstream. They anchored off the mouth of a river they named Cap Rouge. The sailors, who were new to Canada, gazed happily at the grassy meadows and pleasant shade beneath the groves of trees. The July sunshine was ripening the grapes on wild-growing vines. Men wandering ashore began to pick up stones which they thought contained traces of gold.

"Is this the country of fearful snow?" the simple fellows asked jokingly. "Why, the sun shines more warmly here than in France! And where in our own country could we pick up wealth from the ground as we are doing here?"

"Wait," Cartier told them grimly. "You will see this fair country wither and grow icy before many months have passed. We must build a fort on yonder hillside and give it thick walls and a heavy roof. Its name shall be Charlesbourg Royal. Here, on the banks of this river of Cap Rouge, we will plant potatoes, beans, and onions. Yonder trees must be felled and sawed into logs. I tell you, my friends, that when the icy wind from the north blows across this land, you will bless the hard work which gave us firewood and great stores of vegetables."

The fort of Charlesbourg Royal rose on the hillside. Big pine logs, laid horizontally and covered with sheets of bark, formed the walls. Even then, Cartier was not satisfied. He made the men fill the chinks between the logs with tightly packed mud and moss. The stout roof was built at a steep angle so that snow would slide off it to the ground.

"Even for a careful man our Captain worries too much," the toiling sailors complained. "These great walls and fireplaces and stout palisades make one think he is afraid of the cold weather ahead."

The first cold winds of winter scattered the dead leaves and brought flurries of snow. Not an Indian came to the fort with presents of venison or other game. The Huron people of Kebec were still brooding over their friends who had not returned from France. Some-

times an arrow streaked out of the silent forest and buried its bone-tipped point in the walls of the fort. This was the Indian way of showing that the white strangers were no longer welcome in the land of Canada.

The Frenchmen, beginning to grow afraid of this strange, lonely country, peered down the River of Hochelaga. Count Roberval had promised to come before the end of the year. Now patches of ice were forming on the surface of the water. It was unlikely that he would arrive this late. The two hundred men began to realize they would have no extra company for the winter.

"We have nothing to fear," Cartier told them. "We have plenty of meat and the vegetables will keep for a while. When our onions and beans are finished, I will show you how to stay free of scurvy by drinking a brew made from pine trees."

The winter passed slowly. The men slept in bunks around the sides of the fort's great hall, where big iron stoves burned red-hot by day and night. Even so, the temperature in the living quarters dropped to freezing only a few feet from the fires. Outside the fort there was nothing to see except the black forest and white snowdrifts. The men feared to walk beyond the palisade, for no one could guess where an Indian might be lurking among the trees.

The men became bored, restless, and lonely.

Some of them only slept and ate and grumbled. Others fashioned leather garments from the skins of deer they had shot during the summer. A number amused themselves by making snowshoes, carving wooden figures, or casting leaden bullets for their guns. From time to time the men in that lonely fort were terrified by the roar of blizzards. They muttered frightened prayers when they heard the crash of great trees bursting apart from the cold of January nights. All of them said thankfully that but for Captain Cartier's wise advice, they might be dying of cold and scurvy by now.

Spring came at last. The ice on the river melted and green buds appeared on the trees. Each day the sun rose higher in a pale blue sky, and each day the Frenchmen became more eager to return to France.

"Let us go at once," they insisted. "What sense is there in remaining any longer in this land of pitiless winters and lurking enemies. The king has forgotten us and Roberval will not come."

Cartier looked at the angry faces surrounding him. He knew that these weary men were on the point of mutiny. They might decide to take the ships and go, no matter how much he tried to stop them. Perhaps Cartier himself no longer trusted the king's memory or Roberval's promises. He was worried by Indian war parties, which were prowling around the fort in increasing numbers. The Indians might decide to attack at any time. A fight between Frenchmen and Hurons would ruin all chance of making friends with the tribe again.

"Very well," said Cartier. "Make ready the ships."

The five vessels sailed down the St. Lawrence River and reached the Atlantic Ocean in June, 1542. A day or so later Cartier

sighted white sails in the distance. Count Roberval was coming at last to join him in Canada.

The two fleets furled their sails and floated close to one another on the calm sea. Cartier rowed across the water in a small boat and stepped aboard Roberval's vessel.

Among the seamen Cartier recognized the faces of good, honest fellows who had gone fishing with him off the coast of Newfoundland. But crowded on the deck were other passengers whom Cartier did not like the look of.

Roberval was in a friendly mood. He smiled when he saw Cartier gazing at this villainous-looking company. "They are not a handsome crowd," he said. "I could find only a few volunteers for our colony on the shores of the Great River of Canada. The good people of France are not yet willing to risk their lives among the Indians. I had to search elsewhere for these men and women you see now."

"Where did you find them, my lord?" asked Cartier. "In the jails of Paris?"

Roberval nodded. "Most of them. A few were in other prisons. All were serving long terms for various crimes. Some were under sentence of death. I had them pardoned and released, on condition that they sail with me to Canada. At least they will help us build our settlement."

"They may help *you*, perhaps, my lord," Cartier said in a quiet but serious voice. "But I have no wish to see these poor wretches suffer hunger and fear and loneliness. Indeed, it would be kinder to return them to their prisons than to expect them to spend a winter here. So I will continue my voyage to France, my lord. You, I see, are anxious to sail onward to the River of Hochelaga. If the Indians have not destroyed our fort of Charlesbourg Royal, you will find a place to live with these unhappy souls."

Roberval's lean, bad-tempered face became bright with rage. "I order you to return with me," he shouted. "If you refuse, not a penny of the wealth we shall obtain from furs and minerals will ever be yours."

Cartier looked Roberval straight in the eye. "I have spent two winters in Canada. Those with me were better men than most of those you have brought with you. Even so, we were barely able to live, although we planted food and built a fort and kept unsleeping watch by day and night. Do you think, my lord, that your settlers will be able to do better than that? Without handy men and brave women in Charlesbourg Royal, your plans are sure to go wrong. I repeat, my lord, that I intend to go back to France with my ships."

Cartier returned to his vessel. Roberval leaned over the side to shout angry threats at him. The two fleets parted. Roberval's ships moved on toward Canada. Cartier headed eastward across the Atlantic to St. Malo.

Roberval had no pity for the unhappy men and women with him. He treated even his young niece, Marguerite, in a wickedly cruel way. This nineteen-year-old girl had decided to come to Canada in search of adventure. While the ships were passing Newfoundland, Roberval picked a quarrel with her. He ordered a boat to take Marguerite, her old

nurse, and a young sailor to a rocky little
island in the Gulf of St. Lawrence. There
these three unfortunate people were left with
a few blankets, some cooking pots, and a
couple of muskets.

For a while they managed to live on bear
meat, fish, and sea birds. After a few months
the young sailor died. When winter came the
old nurse passed away, and Marguerite was
left alone on the island. Wild bears nosed
around the hut, trying to find a way to de-

vour her. The brave girl drove them off with her musket and ate the flesh of the animals she killed. When summer came she cooked sea birds and boiled handfuls of reedlike grass, which she ate as a green vegetable. Somehow she managed to remain alive for nearly two years.

One day a French schooner came into the Gulf of St. Lawrence. The crew hoped to meet a party of Indians and exchange knives and fishing hooks for furs. A sharp-eyed sailor aboard the ship noticed smoke rising from the island. The schooner changed course and came closer to the shore, where astonished seamen found poor Marguerite, dressed in bearskins, cooking a clumsy meal over a fire. They took her aboard their vessel and returned to France soon afterward.

Meanwhile, Roberval and his two hundred colonists settled down in Fort Charlesbourg Royal in the late summer of 1542.

Roberval bullied the unhappy people from morning to night. The men toiled to plant food, build extra houses, split logs, and strengthen the palisade. Women cooked meals, carried water from the river, made clothes from the skins of wild animals, cleaned the houses, and helped the men with much of the heavier work. Roberval shot or hanged anyone who disobeyed his harsh orders. Nearly every day some poor person was tied to a tree and thrashed. Prisoners were made to wear heavy chains on their ankles while they worked.

The Indians wept when they saw the great suffering of these people. They fired no more arrows, and their war parties left the fort alone. "These people will soon die," the Hurons said to one another. "Their mad leader will destroy them all. Why should we spill our blood by attacking them?"

Perhaps Roberval was a little mad. His

most foolhardy action was to send back the ships which had brought him from France.

Scurvy killed off many of the settlers during the winter. None of them knew how to make medicine from spruce trees, and Cartier was not there to guide and advise them. Less than a hundred people were left alive when spring returned.

In faraway France, good Jacques Cartier rightly guessed what was happening to Roberval and his settlement in Canada. "It is not my affair," he said to a high official who was close to the king. "Yet I think it would be kind to send a ship to the River of Hochelaga. Count Roberval may have changed his mind about remaining in Canada forever."

Ships went out to seek Roberval in the summer of 1543. Cartier himself sailed in command of them. They rescued Roberval, who had lost most of his teeth from scurvy, and those wretched men and women who were still alive. When the ships returned down the river, not a single Frenchman was left in Canada.

Grave-faced Indians watched the ships go sailing past. They grunted with satisfaction and returned to their bark houses in the village of Stadacona. The white men have gone away at last, they thought. They did not know how to live in this country of ours, for they were clumsy at fishing and almost useless at hunting. Now perhaps they will stay for always in their strange country across the Bitter Water.

For a while it seemed as if the Huron warriors were right. Almost fifty years were to pass before other Frenchmen would come to build new forts on the open meadows below the high gray cliffs. Until then silence returned to the forests. Only the slender keels of birch-bark canoes disturbed the surface of the Great River of Canada.

No one knows what happened to Roberval. One story says that he made a second voyage to Canada some years later, but that his ship sank during an Atlantic storm. Other stories say he was shot and killed one night in Paris. Perhaps one of the men he treated cruelly in Fort Charlesbourg Royal aimed the pistol.

Cartier's exploring days were over. The war against Spain was going badly. The king needed every man and ship he could get. He lost interest in Canada when French experts declared that the diamonds Cartier's men had brought back were worthless crystals of quartz. And he had learned that the gold the colonists had picked up beside the St. Lawrence was only a kind of iron ore.

But King Francis remembered to be grateful to that honest little sea captain, Jacques Cartier. "You found a way into the heart of a great new country," the king said to him. "You discovered the River of Hochelaga, as

you named it. And what is more, good Captain Cartier, you were always honest in the news you brought back to us. All these things you have done faithfully and at the risk of your life. Go back to your native town of St. Malo. Until the end of your days you shall receive a pension from me, my friend Cartier."

Fifty-year-old Jacques Cartier spent the last six years of his life where he could see and hear the Atlantic Ocean. From the front window of his stone house he could watch the sun go down in the west.

"There'll be dark shadows spreading soon across the land of Canada," he would say to his old seafaring friends. "I remember how the gloom of those great pine forests grows darker with the approach of night. The Indians' fires will be burning brightly in Stadacona and in the village of Hochelaga, beneath Mount Royal. Maybe those painted savages will be dancing tonight to the thud of their great drums. Aye, yonder is a great country, my friends. Yet its cold and loneliness will break the hearts of many men before towns and farms and forts stand close to where once I sailed along that mighty river."